UNLOCKING WALL ART MAGIC: A Comprehensive Guide to Elevate Your Home Decor

Meghan Brooke

Table of Contents

CHAPTER ONE

INTRODUCTION

Plans make a game-plan nature that adds tone and an invigorating energy to the home. An unimaginable viewpoint concerning blaming up for plans is that they can be used with a style. You ought to just pick the ones that go with the rest of your tangled connection.

The fundamental sorts of models used for restoring a home set plant, subject and numerical. The standard models make a tricky, strengthened elaborate connection those lights up the room. These make a more standard or old style shift center over to the home.

FURTHER MAKING WALL CLOCK

A wall clock is potentially of the most practical and unprecedented piece in any home. With the improvement being made, huge level watches have turned out to be unquestionable yet the obvious thought of wall tickers has not diminished. Surely, even today overwhelmingly most slope toward standard plans as it pours out over an extraordinary appeal and dazzling elegance. Standard tickers with minute hands and second hands are involved even in schools so youths can sort out a decent strategy for overseeing exactly give without holding down anything that time it is. Wall tickers are both essential and blaming up for its charming shapes and styles.

METAL CRAFTSMANSHIP

It has changed into a popular manual for extra develop homes, bistros, lodgings, ranches and stops with custom metal workmanship overhauls. Metal plans of the typical western culture are the most in regular elaborate thing for doing in that limit. It is central for re-endeavor the updates so they network nearby the standard parts. The metal parts should exist together with the normal parts where they are used. The use of metal workmanship is in a way giving us back the energy of the well established standard plans. It licenses us to taste the presence of our forerunners by having their outside and inside home beautifications in our homes.

MIRRORS

Mirrors are a basic piece of home style as it manages the interior bits of the room in more than one way. More undeniable home style mirrors can do thinks about especially when you have little dwelling space. They reflect light and groupings thusly making a space have the stores of being all huger and inconceivably more noticeable than it genuinely is. Mirrors are found in flood keeping watch. The basic thing to study while really focusing in on the ideal one for your home, you should close whether you should go for standing mirrors or wall mirrors. In case you have a little space, wall mirrors are perfect for your walls.

WALL VERBALIZATIONS

Wall craftsmanship fundamentally proposes a quality gem usually hung or done on the wall. Such an imaginative work routinely adds more tone and importance to the house where it's shown. Each person who very to complete their home ought to go for fair gems that could be painted or held tight the wall.

BEWILDERING KINDS OF EXTRAVAGANT WALL WORKMANSHIP FOR YOUR HOME

When you hear the word craftsmanship, what picture skips into your mind? For an enormous part of us, we think about a scene or picture. With everything considered, we a critical piece of the time use the word craftsmanship and painting of course. Clearly, workmanship can solidify various media, similar to figures, depicts, and so forth. One of the most beguiling combinations of craftsmanship is wall workmanship. We could take out this general depiction of craftsmanship, into sub-classes. If you are mulling over adding wall craftsmanship to the walls of any room, then, at that point, contemplate these principal sorts:

1. Wall grilles

Considering everything, people have involved grilles as an extra shield for windows and segments. In any case, wall grilles limit totally for beautification. Two or three grilles are an effect from the past, resembling styles during occasions like the Incredible or Renaissance period. Meanwhile, various grilles have a more contemporary soul. There are goliath grilles, little grilles, round grilles, and tall grilles.

2. Wall wine rack

You can use this partner with pieces paying minimal admonition to wine bottles! Select a wine rack for one compartment, or one for various holders. Pick a style that is basically even, or one that is more luxurious. Whether you favor red or white wine, use this kind of amazing wall workmanship to show your wine bottles in style!

3. Wall holders

Holders should occur with relax region tables and workspaces, right? With wall surprise, the compartment moves from the one level surface, to another level surface unequivocally, the wall. Wall holders can take in new live into any wall, without assistance from another individual or stacked down with adolescents and foliage. You can pick a compartment (or match) that sees a showstopper of the past, or one with a smoother and contemporary look.

4. Wall racks

If you genuinely need a rack with more adaptability than a rack, consider a wall rack. These racks fit securely on a wall, and are open in a wide combination of styles. There are wall racks from various periods, including out of date Greek and Roman, Renaissance, and Gothic. You can upgrade these phenomenal pieces with a light, compartment photograph any knickknack that you really need to present to your visitors!

5. Wall tickers

These tickers keep unbelievable time the entire day. Instead of picking a dull mechanized clock, select a manual clock that tells you the time as well as does it with style! These watches are available in various shapes, sizes, and styles. Two or three combinations of this breathing new live into wall workmanship have a bound appearance, while others are more unusual.

6. Wall shadowboxes

The first shadowboxes are ones that the key obliges sailors, upon their leaving the boat or taking out the military. A wall shadowbox is by and large a tight sort of box that contains a picture or pointlessness in it. The three layered part can add more basic significance to any wall in your home. Expecting you want to add wall expressive arrangement to your walls, you have several options, including wooden wall craftsmanship. Endeavor to pick everything watchfully, to ensure that you room has finish wrapping up!

CHAPTER TWO

WALL CRAFTSMANSHIP AND COMPLEX STRATEGY

Wall craftsmanship and style is essential in your home since, workmanship helps set the general perspective of its not unexpected parts. Workmanship expressive arrangement to some degree shows your style and allows you to make your home a home, changing each room with a creation or picture. Adding style tone and energy to each wall will give your home individual. Before you hang those materials and pictures endeavor to pick the disposition setting that you really need for your home, watching out for style and assortment. Each room should be done one more framework for showing what the room is used for. Whether it is the parlor region or the youths play room, it's pivotal setting the attitude. There are different inclinations that your home can feel like, in view of wall workmanship and expressive subject. While picking a demeanor consider picture position, and the mix devise you genuinely need to use. Different groupings can make the room express might we at any point at some point stone or time to relax. Persisting through you see the getting district ought to feel warm and inviting, you should have an earth changed hidden wall, with pictures held up over the kinship seat, that are fumbling and astonishing. In the event that you essentially want to make the kid's room send an impression of being Fun and stunning have a hitting stowed away wall with photos of youngster's shows hung out of control. The style of the room is additionally gigantic while going with the decision of what kind of craftsmanship expressive alliance you should place in the room and where you should put it. In case you have current styled furniture, in a dull gathering you should hang present day fair pieces and shockingly isolating pictures, wall craftsmanship and elaborate connection is used to work with a room and show class and multi-layered nature in this style of room. Style of furniture and the spot of furniture is a basic piece of going with the decision of what kind of craftsmanship to have. While hanging, or spreading out pictures in a room, position is the last decision yet the most obvious to make. Putting pictures on an uncovered wall or incredibly over a veneration seat will clearly stand out and start a conversation when you have affiliation. While spreading out a picture onto a wall it is for each situation eminent to at first draw the picture out with a pencil first, thusly if you influence your point of view it won't mean a repaint of the walls. With a picture or piece of craftsmanship above plans or on an evident wall, either beating a nail into the wall or using pushpins, is the most un-perilous and most standard way.

While completing a house wall workmanship and style is the best system for testing things up or chill things. With a sprinkle of style and blend coordination you will make your home feel how you pick. Bringing conversation and energy workmanship work not just communicates the kind of individual you craftsmanship, yet in addition shows your child of style.. Fine art is the least complex method for changing a whole room, by putting an image on an exposed wall you have added a genuinely new thing for the eye to get.

WALL WORKMANSHIP WOVEN ARTWORKS THOUGHTS FOR WALL STYLISTIC THEME

Choosing wall workmanship for your home can be an exceptionally intriguing cycle. Whether you're enhancing your home interestingly, or remodeling a home, wall workmanship will add warmth and character to your home. So where do you begin?

Happy you inquired! An extraordinary spot to start to be know all about the decisions you have as wall craftsmanship as stylistic layout. Wall embroideries are a type of wall craftsmanship that is as famous today as anyone might imagine.

They're utilized by home producers and craftsmanship darlings the same, and their woven surface adds a glow and presence to any home. So how would you involve wall workmanship woven artworks as wall stylistic layout for your home? The following are 3 sorts or subjects of craftsmanship woven artworks you can use to enrich your home:

STILL LIFE CRAFTSMANSHIP WOVEN ARTWORKS

Still life embroidered works of art have been a famous decision for stylistic layout for quite a long time. The topic natural product, blossoms, containers and wine have been a most loved subject for craftsmen, including notable Dutch and other European painters. Still life craftsmanship can incredibly affect our faculties. The utilization of light and the brilliant shades of the blossoms can truly rejuvenate a room. Still life workmanship woven artworks include huge detail and nearly look genuine. They carry the magnificence of nature to within our homes, and for this reason still lives are as yet utilized as home stylistic layout.

SCENE OR LANDSCAPE EMBROIDERIES

Scenes and landscape embroideries are one more type of wall craftsmanship for the home. These workmanship pieces come in many styles, from exceptionally itemized scenes of laborers working in the fields, to peaceful scenes showing couples in affection. A few embroideries are simply 'verdures' or rich foliage settings with others join components of design with nurseries of renowned French castles. They are novel in that these tapestries give a feeling of presence and climate to any room or home stylistic layout, nearly adding the feeling of this a different universe to your home.

CHAPTER THREE

CURRENT OR CONTEMPORARY WORKMANSHIP EMBROIDERIES

Current workmanship embroideries offer something for everybody, from country scenes to present day plans, from portieres to current occasions. These works are unimaginably shifted in their topic, style and expressionism. Some craftsmanship embroideries made in the contemporary structure could undoubtedly balance in the absolute best current workmanship historical centers in America. There are a wide assortment of plans to suit practically any creative taste and inclinations.

So that's it.

These are 3 sorts of wall craftsmanship embroidered works of art which can be utilized as home and wall stylistic theme. While choosing wall workmanship for your home, select works that address you and which give a general feel that you need for your home stylistic theme. Designing a room from to improve your room setting can be an extremely thrilling undertaking. While picking wall craftsmanship, pick a piece that addresses you and which will improve your home setting.

ORNAMENTAL REMOVABLE AND REUSABLE WALL WORKMANSHIP

Improving your home can be a great deal of work and, surprisingly, more work to fix it when the opportunity arrives for a change. There is painting adhering and sanding also fixing up walls assuming you harms them all the while. Be that as it may, embellishing doesn't need to make your home a building site. Utilizing removable wall stickers permits you to have the opportunity of enriching without the entirety of the difficult work. There is an extensive variety of beautifying wall workmanship accessible that is reasonable for any room in the home, including removable and reusable wall stickers and imaginative customized wall craftsmanship. Assuming you are improving your kid's room search for beautiful stickers that are non harmful PVC vinyl, self cement and removable. They permit you to move and eliminate them without stripping off paint or leaving any buildup behind when taken out.

A scope of removable and reusable glue stickers for youngster's rooms and nurseries are accessible and incorporate creature, blackboard, level diagram, space and vehicles topics. The creature wall decals can be utilized for both young men and young ladies rooms and proposition a scope of plans and course of action choices. The creature tower level outline wall decal is great for engaging developing kids while the blackboard wall stickers give a tomfoolery space to be inventive with chalk. The Trains, planes and vehicle wall stickers can add experience to any young men rooms while the young ladies can partake in the beautiful butterfly themed garden wall stickers.

Notwithstanding nursery wall stickers and ornamental decals, there is a scope of imaginative customized child prints for the nursery. The prints arrive in a scope of sizes and are in many cases uniquely crafted per request. They are customized to frequently include the singular child's name, date of birth, season of birth along with choices to modify the casing and text tone. No two prints will be the equivalent in view of your child's singular subtleties, giving an exceptional answer for nursery embellishments. The customized name print includes only the kid's name and is great for the two children rooms and nurseries. For different rooms in the home the wall workmanship providers offer a determination of lovely and exquisite wall decals. There are garden wall stickers that incorporate varieties like birds, blossoms, trees and examples. The blossom bird's wall stickers are ladylike yet adaptable with wonderful birds and proclamations blossoms can light up the home. These embellishing decals are self cement and removable and the plans can be all organized in various ways of fitting the wall space. Ideal for the residing or feasting region they are a brilliant expansion reasonable for any room in the home. Most improving stickers can be effectively applied by the kids with the assistance of a grown-up as the self cement plans are easy to apply requiring no additional paste for application.

The semi-super durable nature of the removable wall stickers mean the client isn't limited to one format plan or expected to repaint the walls to change the appearance of the room. The singular sticker application implies their course of action can be customized to suit each room, youngster or inclination. The plans are easy to strip off and don't harm the wall or the paint all the while.

The removable and reusable wall craftsmanship and customized prints give a straightforward and lovely answer for home enhancing. The removable and reusable glue wall stickers give the opportunity of eliminating or moving the wall stickers without harming the paint as well as the adaptability of putting the stickers in different ways making them one of a kind to each wall. The customized prints give one more one of a kind arrangement by permitting the print to be totally extraordinary to the room and youngster. So whenever you are adorning consider the straightforward arrangement of enhancing wall workmanship and removable wall stickers to carry life to your walls without the problem.

SORTS OF METAL WALL CRAFTSMANSHIP

There are many styles of metal craftsmanship you can buy to decorate your walls. There are a few unique completes that you can have on the piece, including cast iron or bronze. Nonetheless, there are unmistakable types of metal wall workmanship that you can find: practical and improving.

Practical wall workmanship is pieces that really fill a need in your home. This could be anything from wall sconces, wellsprings, key racks and that's only the tip of the iceberg. These things are made to look wonderful as well as to fill a need you might require for the room.

Improving wall craftsmanship then again is essentially a piece of workmanship that is on your walls to upgrade the room by giving it a certain style. Metal workmanship arrives in a wide range of structures that can be molded after creatures, individuals or even theoretical items.

CHAPTER FOUR

WHERE TO TRACK DOWN METAL WORKMANSHIP

Assuming you honestly love metal wall workmanship, you should know where you can find the piece you are searching for. Incredibly, it tends to be found at practically any store that sells brightening things. This incorporates places, for example, retail chains as well as workmanship exhibitions. Contingent upon the sort of piece you are searching for there are better places you should go. At the point when you go into a home improvement or retail chain, you will find an alternate sort of wall craftsmanship than what you would find at a display. Assuming you are searching for a practical piece of workmanship that is more modest and on the more affordable side, your smartest option is to pick a corporate retailer that sells things for the home. These things are efficiently manufactured, which permits them to be sold at lower costs.

Nonetheless, assuming you are searching for a piece from a famous craftsman that will offer a delightful and intense expression about you and your home, then you should visit a workmanship display or sale. These can be extraordinary spots to find exceptional bits of metal wall craftsmanship.

EFFECTIVE METHOD TO MAKE YOUR OWN TEXTURE WALL CRAFTSMANSHIP

Wall workmanship and wall style don't need to be just about artworks as well as photos. That is the more customary way to deal with embellishing walls. Texture wall decorations, in any case, can truly make a room more improving and truly add an individual touch to your finishing subject. Perhaps now is the ideal time to consider involving some texture in your next designing undertaking? There's such countless various ways of making this kind of wall workmanship panic don't as well in the event that you don't have the foggiest idea where to begin. How far you go with this will rely totally upon what your creative leanings are and how long you can put resources into the actual undertaking. Certain individuals are happy with genuinely straightforward wall workmanship, while others track down it enjoyable to invest a ton of energy making their own novel piece of wall craftsmanship. One of the fastest and most straightforward ways of making texture wall workmanship is simply to find a plan that you are partial to, a then to extend it over a casing. You can then drape this piece of texture craftsmanship in your room easily. As a matter of fact, this will wind up very closely resembling another composition or picture however have that additional bit of style to it from being made with texture. This is something worth being thankful for to do assuming you have a blanket that you like yet don't use consistently. You can take all or part of the blanket, and edge it to make your new masterpiece. Another choice, obviously, is simply to track down embroidery and hang it up. In any case, it very well may be generally elusive embroidered works of art except if you're prone to track down things like this.

Different instances of texture tapestries that you can search for are costly or itemized cover. There are a few covers that are lovely to such an extent that they will brighten any wall in any room. This could sound a gnawed off the wall yet it merits examining.

In the event that you have additional opportunity to spend on your wall craftsmanship, you should think about doing some weaving. You can either weave your own plan, or you can find a unit that makes it extremely simple to assemble a weaved picture on a piece of texture. One way or the other this will provide you with a really novel piece of wall craftsmanship for your (or a companions) home.

A great many people who are into weaving will observe that this is a pleasant method for making embellishing wall craftsmanship. Weaving can be exceptionally tedious yet the end-product is dependably worth the work.

METHODS FOR HANGING AND ORGANIZING WALL WORKMANSHIP STYLISTIC LAYOUT

Make a grandstand of warmth and character to any room by changing your wall style. Adding a course of action of outlined photos, mirrors, wall figures, and collectibles is a reasonable method for changing any room in your home. Here are a few methods for organizing and hanging your wall workmanship with certainty. Orchestrating Your Craft: The objective while organizing wall workmanship is to make a satisfying visual presentation that exhibits it.

To design your format, cut out butcher paper layouts a similar size and shape as the wall style you need to hang. Tape them on the wall with veiling tape, moving them around as you would prefer. Mark the positions gently with a pencil on the wall. You may likewise orchestrate your work of art on the floor agreeable to you prior to nailing to the wall.

Bunch your specialty as per theme. Create a showcase by gathering the things by topic rehashing tones and styles of the room's inside.

Bunch comparative things and make a balanced shape. The key to organizing wall craftsmanship is to accomplish balance. For instance, little pictures held tight a huge wall can watch out of equilibrium and will seem lost in an untamed ocean of room. On the off chance that you have a bigger work of art or mirror, it has sufficient presence to remain solitary on an enormous wall. Evenness adds balance and is for the most part exceptionally satisfying to the onlooker.

On the off chance that you need to bring down your craftsmanship to repaint, snap a picture of your plan so you can return it simply how it was. Hanging Your Specialty: Instruments you will require are a mallet, level, measuring tape, picture holders or nails you've likely consistently heard that fine art ought to be hung so the middle mark of the image or gathering is about eye level for the typical level of an individual A decent spot to begin is to hang the piece roughly 60-65 creeps from the floor to the focal point of the workmanship. Pieces ought to be hung roughly 6 crawls over a mantle or rack. Try not to leave a huge void space among workmanship and furniture. There ought to be a 10 inch leeway above couches and headboards.

While draping workmanship over a household item, it ought not to be longer than the width of the furnishings.

Assuming that the craftsmanship weighs five pounds or more, utilize two walls secures per painting to equally disseminate the weight. The image will hang all the more uniformly, too.

To safeguard your wall and keep the image from moving, append felt cushions to the base corners on the rear of the edge. When done accurately, hanging wall workmanship is a fast, simple and reasonable method for adding influence and revives your home.

THE END

www.ingramcontent.com/pod-product-compliance
Lightning Source LLC
Chambersburg PA
CBHW070741260726
48660CB00007B/2931